How Do Cell Phones Work?

by Richard Hantula

**Science and Curriculum Consultant: Debra Voege, M.A.,
Science Curriculum Resource Teacher**

CHELSEA
CLUBHOUSE
An Imprint of Chelsea House Publishers

Science in the Real World: How Do Cell Phones Work?

Chelsea Clubhouse
An imprint of Chelsea House Publishers
132 West 31st Street
New York NY 10001

Library of Congress Cataloging-in-Publication Data
Hantula, Richard.
        How do cell phones work? / by Richard Hantula; science and curriculum consultant, Debra Voege.
            p. cm. — (Science in the real world)
        Includes index.
        ISBN 978-1-60413-475-9
        1. Cellular telephones—Juvenile literature. I. Title.
    TK6570.M6H278 2009
    621.3845'6—dc22   2009002167

Chelsea Clubhouse books are available at special discounts when purchased in bulk quantities for businesses, associations, institutions, or sales promotions. Please call our Special Sales Department in New York at (212) 967-8800 or (800) 322-8755.

You can find Chelsea Clubhouse on the World Wide Web at http://www.chelseahouse.com

Developed for Chelsea House by RJF Publishing LLC (www.RJFpublishing.com)
Text and cover design by Tammy West/Westgraphix LLC
Illustrations by Spectrum Creative Inc.
Photo research by Edward A. Thomas
Index by Nila Glikin

Photo Credits: cover: Shutterstock Images; 4: Comstock Images/JUPITERIMAGES; 5: Andersen Ross/Brand X Pictures/JUPITERIMAGES; 6: Ericsson's Historical Archives/Centre for Business History, Stockholm; 7, 8, 28: AP/Wide World Photos; 12, 15, 18, 19, 21: iStockphoto; 16, 23: Alamy; 22: Goodshoot/JUPITERIMAGES; 24, 26: © Nokia Corporation; 25: Tess Shannon; 29: Continental Airlines.

Printed and bound in the United States of America

Bang RJF 10 9 8 7 6 5 4 3 2 1

This book is printed on acid-free paper.

All links and Web addresses were checked and verified to be correct at the time of publication. Because of the dynamic nature of the Web, some addresses and links may have changed since publication and may no longer be valid.

Table of Contents

Words that are defined in the Glossary are in **bold** type
the first time they appear in the text.

Changing the Way We Live

Some people call it a mobile phone. Some use the name "wireless phone." Some say "cell phone." Some just say "cell." No matter what you call it, it is a marvel.

Some cell phones weigh as little as 3 to 4 ounces (85 to 113 grams)—they are lighter than a bar of soap. Some are less than 4 inches (10 centimeters) long. These little gadgets can do millions of things a second. They turn speech into electric signals and turn signals into speech. They send the signals as radio waves, and they receive radio waves. They link up with phone **networks**. They have a

Many cell phones take pictures and do a lot of other things besides making calls.

memory. Most cell phones have games. Many play music, take pictures, and record video. Some can surf the Web.

No More Wires

Cell phones have changed how people live. Years ago, telephones were big. Most were used just for talking. Almost all of them needed a wire to connect to the telephone network. To make a call, you had to go to where a phone was—and sometimes even wait in line to use it! Today, your cell phone goes with you. You can make a call almost anywhere. Also, since a cell phone does lots of other things, these things can all be done most anywhere too. Cell phones make people able to work and have fun in new ways.

Cell phones let you stay in touch almost anywhere.

DID YOU KNOW ?

Mighty Mite

A cell phone can be as small as it is because it is built like a computer. It is full of tiny devices called **transistors**. Years ago there were no transistors. Glass bulbs called vacuum tubes were used instead. If a cell phone had vacuum tubes, it would be as big as the Washington Monument!

Radios were invented more than 100 years ago. Radios that let you both talk and listen are called two-way radios. Early two-way radio sets were huge. By the 1930s there were sets that fit in a police car. Smaller sizes came later.

The **walkie-talkie**, for example, is small enough to carry. It lets you do one thing at a time: talk or listen. It links to another walkie-talkie. It does not link to a phone. The first ones were made in the early 1940s, and

A mobile phone from the 1950s. Large and heavy, phones like this were mostly put in cars.

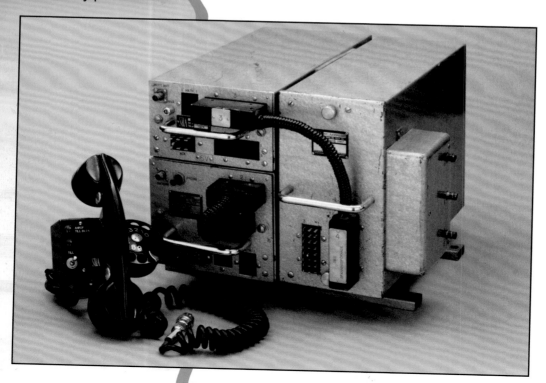

at that time, they were used by soldiers in World War II.

There was a public mobile phone system in St. Louis, Missouri, by 1946. It did not work well, but people already dreamed of tiny radios and phones. The comic strip detective Dick Tracy had a wristwatch with a two-way radio in it.

The First Hand-Held Phones

By 1973 there was a mobile phone you could hold in your hand. It was bigger than a brick, though not quite as heavy. It was 10 inches (25 centimeters) long and 3 inches (7.6 cm) thick, and it weighed 2 pounds (0.9 kilograms).

Cell phones then grew smaller. They first became popular in Japan and Europe. In the United States they caught on more slowly.

DID YOU KNOW ?

Hand Held

Many people helped invent cell phones. Martin Cooper (above) was one. He worked at the American company Motorola. In 1973 he made the first wireless phone that could be held in one hand, and he also made the first call from his "**handset**."

Big Business

Today, cell phones are everywhere. They first went on sale in the United States in 1983. By 1995, just 12 years later, Americans had 28 million cell phones. By 2008 they had more than 260 million. Some homes don't have a **landline phone** anymore. (Landline phones use a wire to link to the phone network.) People just use their cell phones, whether they're out or at home.

The story is much the same elsewhere. In Africa cell phones are more popular than landlines. In 2007 the world had 3.3 billion cell phones. That means one phone for every two

Cell phones are the most popular kind of phones in Africa. Here, Wangari Maathai of Kenya takes a call to congratulate her after she won the 2004 Nobel Peace Prize for her work to save the environment and protect women's rights.

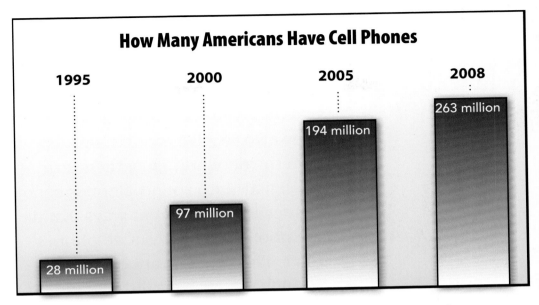

How Many Americans Have Cell Phones

1995 — 28 million
2000 — 97 million
2005 — 194 million
2008 — 263 million

people. This number is an average. Some areas had few phones. Some had many.

Who Makes Cell Phones

Most cell phones are made by a few giant companies. As of 2007, the top company was Nokia. It is based in Finland. More than 1 billion cell phones were made in the world in 2007. Nokia made two out of every five of them—more than 400 million phones. The number-two company in 2007 was Samsung. It is based in South Korea. The number-three company was Motorola. Samsung made more than 160 million phones. Motorola made almost as many.

Radio Links

All telephones turn sound into electric signals. They send the signals to the telephone network. They also receive electric signals from the network. They then turn the signals into sound. Phones send and receive in different ways. Landline phones use wires. Cell phones don't. Their signals are carried through the air by radio waves.

Radio waves are **electromagnetic radiation**. This is a way energy moves from one place to another. Ordinary light is a form of it. So are the invisible types of light called **infrared** and ultraviolet (ultraviolet light from the sun causes sunburn). X-rays that dentists and doctors use are another form. Electromagnetic radiation has waves. In water waves, the water goes up and down. Radio waves and light waves also have ups and downs. They are connected with energy. Each type of wave has a number called the **frequency**. This is the number of ups and downs, or cycles, that occur each second. One cycle per second is called 1 **hertz**.

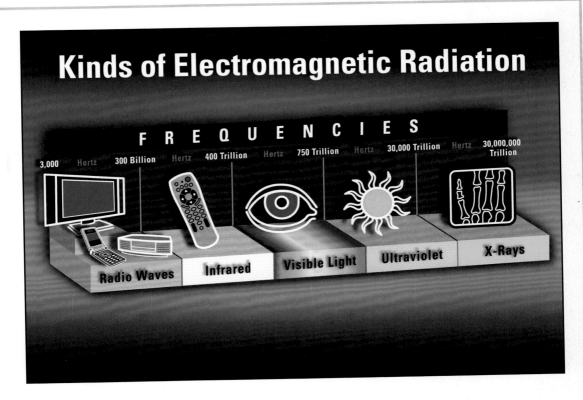

Kinds of Electromagnetic Radiation

FREQUENCIES

| 3,000 Hertz | 300 Billion Hertz | 400 Trillion Hertz | 750 Trillion Hertz | 30,000 Trillion Hertz | 30,000,000 Trillion |

Radio Waves · **Infrared** · **Visible Light** · **Ultraviolet** · **X-Rays**

Cell Phone Frequencies

Radio waves have frequencies between 3,000 hertz and 300 billion hertz (or ups and downs per second). Waves with frequencies within this range are used for a lot of purposes. Broadcast radio and television are examples. Cell phones are another. Each purpose uses only certain frequencies within the range.

Different kinds of electromagnetic radiation have very different frequencies.

DID YOU KNOW ?

Analog and Digital

Early cell phones used **analog** signals. Today's cell phones mostly use **digital** signals. Analog signals are similar, or "analogous," to the original sound. With digital, the sound is chopped up into tiny bits of information. These bits are then sent. Digital signals can use a smaller band of frequencies than analog. They also are easier to work with.

Standards

A cell phone signal can be put into radio waves in more than one way. Different cell phone networks use different methods. A phone might not work with certain networks. It depends on what method the network uses. It also depends on what methods the phone can handle. The most widely used method is GSM. Its name means "global system for mobile communications." It is used in most

Many people use their cell phone for texting—that is, for sending text messages.

of the world. Some U.S. networks use it. Other methods have names like FDMA, CDMA, and TDMA.

New Generations

Cell phones have come in stages called generations. Early cell phones used analog signals. They are first-generation, or "1G," phones.

The use of digital signals marked the second generation. Such "2G" phones began to show up in the 1990s. Digital signals made it possible for cell phone users to send and receive data (for example, e-mail) as well as make phone calls.

Third-generation, or "3G," phones send and receive signals at very high speeds. Many of these 3G phones can easily surf the Internet or make video calls.

DID YOU KNOW ?

Push-to-Talk

A cell phone is a fancy two-way radio. It uses different frequencies for outgoing and incoming sound. Unlike a walkie-talkie, it lets you talk and hear at the same time. Some phones, however, can also work like a walkie-talkie. This is often called push-to-talk. By pushing a button you can quickly connect with someone. That person must also have a phone with this feature.

The Cell

The "cell" in "cell phone" refers to how you link to the telephone network. The large area served by a cell phone company is divided up into small pieces called **cells**. Each cell has a site called a **base station**. This station has a low-power antenna that sends and receives signals to and from phones in the cell area.

If you make a call, your phone links up with the base station. The station sends your call to a switching center. The call may then be sent to the general telephone network, to be

This picture shows how a cell phone call picked up by a base station antenna is sent to someone's land-line phone.

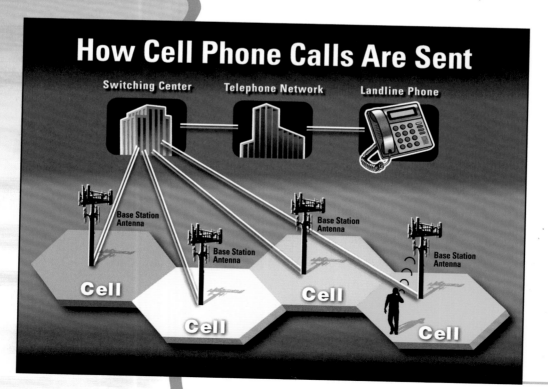

How Cell Phone Calls Are Sent

Switching Center   Telephone Network   Landline Phone

Base Station Antenna

Base Station Antenna

Base Station Antenna

Base Station Antenna

Cell

Cell

Cell

Cell

sent on to the phone that should receive it. If someone calls you, the call goes to your base station, which sends the call to you. This is done very quickly. If you move from one cell area to the next while on a call, the system easily deals with the shift. It hands your call off to the base station in the new cell. You don't notice a thing.

Why Calls Get Dropped

Sometimes, however, calls fail—you can't make your call or your call gets dropped. This can happen if you are too far from the nearest base station. Also, a signal may be blocked by something between you and the base station, such as a building or a hill. Entering a tunnel or an elevator are common reasons why calls get dropped.

Each "cell" of a mobile phone service area has a base station with an antenna like this one.

Before the Cell

Early mobile telephones were limited. There were no cells. A tall, high-power antenna sent and received signals over a big area. Each mobile phone had to have a different frequency. So only a few phones could be used in the area. If you moved outside the area while making a call, your call would be dropped.

More Ways to Connect

Cell phones connect with a base station to send or receive calls or data. Many can also link up with a nearby computer or other device in order to get or send data. One way to connect to a computer is with a cable. There are also wireless methods of connecting. Two common ones use radio waves. They are called Bluetooth and Wi-Fi. Another wireless method is infrared.

This woman has a headset. It frees her hands so she can work on her computer while talking on her cell phone.

Bluetooth works over a short distance. You might use it to connect your phone with a computer or with a headset. The headset has both a microphone and earphones and lets you use the phone without needing to hold it in your hand. Wi-Fi uses more power than Bluetooth. Also, it works over longer distances. Wireless home computer networks use it. A cell phone with Wi-Fi may be able to use it to link to the Web and even make calls over the Internet.

Using Infrared

Infrared is another short-distance method. TV remote controls use infrared. If your cell phone and computer can handle infrared, they can probably connect. You need to point your phone at the computer. Infrared can be blocked by an object between the phone and the computer.

DID YOU KNOW ?

Other Portable Phones

"Wireless phone" usually means "cell phone." But there are other telephones that don't use a wire. "Cordless" phones have handsets that use radio waves to link with a landline. They can't be taken far from the landline. "Satellite phones" can be used almost anywhere. They link up with a satellite in space instead of with a cell base station. They are costly to buy and use.

Key Parts

Nearly all cell phones have certain basic parts. On the outside, there usually is a screen. This can show telephone numbers and messages. It may be able to show pictures as well. The outside also has controls. These are used to make the phone do things. There often is a keypad, or small keyboard. This lets you type numbers, messages, and so on. There may be buttons for special tasks. One button may turn the phone on and off. Other buttons may start or end a call. There may be a scroll wheel or similar control that lets you move around on the screen. Some cell phones let you control the phone by touching the screen.

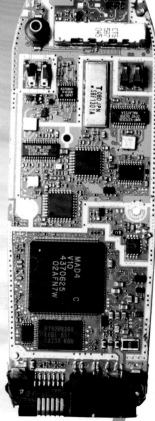

The inside of a cell phone is packed with electronic parts.

Packed with Parts

The inside is packed with parts. One is the microphone. This picks up sound, such as the sound of your voice when you talk. Another is the speaker. It makes sound, so that you can hear the person talking to you. Most phones have a device that can make the phone vibrate, or shake, instead of (or in addition to) ringing to let you know when a call comes in. All phones have a battery. This gives the phone the electricity it needs to work. There also is a small board called a circuit board. It is like the circuit board in a computer. It holds electronic **chips**. These are bits of special material containing tiny devices such as transistors. For the phone to work, it has to process electric signals. One or more chips handle this task. There may be a chip or two that does the job of remembering information. The circuit board also holds circuits—paths along which electricity flows to and from the chips and other parts of the phone. Most phones have a SIM card. "SIM" stands for "subscriber identity module." It tells the network who owns the phone. It may also provide space for storing information such as names and phone numbers.

SIM cards are very small. Look at how much bigger this phone is than the SIM card lying on it.

DID YOU KNOW ?

Where Is the Antenna?

Since it uses radio waves, the phone needs an antenna. In early cell phones, this was on the outside. Today it tends to be inside, but some phones still have antennas that stick out of the top.

Inside and Out

The circuits and devices in a cell phone do many things with electric signals. One example is the system known as a codec. It may have one or more chips. The name comes from "COder" and "DECoder." A codec changes signals from one type to another. It also works in the other direction. In a cell phone, it changes analog signals to digital, and digital to analog.

This is done, for example, in dealing with sound. When sound is picked up by a cell phone's microphone, it is first turned into analog electric signals. These signals have a pattern similar to the sound. Also, when a cell phone's speaker makes sound, it uses analog signals similar to the sound.

On the other hand, when today's cell phones link with a base station, they use digital signals. These are tiny chopped up bits of information. So analog needs to be converted to digital, and digital to analog. All of this is done inside the phone by the phone's codec system.

Some phones flip open (center). In another type (left), one part slides over another. In a candy bar phone (right), the screen and keyboard are on top of a thin block.

What Makes the Phone Vibrate

Some of the jobs done by a phone's devices and circuits involve working with the body of the phone. This may happen, for example, when a call comes in. If your phone is set to vibrate, the call makes a tiny motor start spinning. A weight is attached to the motor. The movement of the weight makes the phone shake.

DID YOU KNOW ?

Candy Bar or Clamshell?

Cell phones come in different forms. The simplest is the bar. This type is also called a candy bar. The screen and keyboard are on top of a thin block. A second type is the clamshell, or flip. It has two halves on a hinge. You open up the phone to use it. You close it when you are done. A third type is the slide. This also has two halves. One slides over the other. A fourth type is the swivel. It has two halves as well. They are attached at one point. One half swings over the other.

Features Galore

Some cell phones do calls but not much more. Other phones do a lot more. They might have an FM radio or a camera, for example. Some are powerful enough to do some of the things that a computer does. These are often called **smart phones**. There also are phones able to store large collections of music. They usually have good sound quality. They are called music phones.

GPS in Cell Phones

A common feature is GPS. "GPS" stands for "Global Positioning System." This is a group of space satellites that give out special radio signals. A normal GPS **receiver** uses these signals to tell its location and

Many people enjoy listening to music on their phones.

the time. Most cell phones sold in the United States in recent years have a simple GPS. It reports location only when the phone is used to call 911 for an emergency. Normal GPS receivers can tell location at any time. Some are used to provide driving directions. Most cell phones can't do all this unless you get an extra receiver device and buy special software or subscribe to a service. Only a few cell phones have a complete GPS receiver.

Smart phones are very handy for business-people on the go.

DID YOU KNOW ?

Personality Plus

Changing the way a phone looks or sounds is easy. Putting on a new cover or faceplate can give it a new personality. Lots of people make their phone stand out by picking a distinctive ring tone—the sound the phone makes when a call arrives (if the phone is set to ring). Usually you can also change the background picture in the phone's screen.

Applications

Applications are what you can do with a cell phone. Three basic things make these activities possible: hardware, software, and services.

Like a computer, a cell phone has hardware and software. The phone's parts make up the hardware. The programs that tell the parts what to do are the software.

These two things are often all you need to use your phone. Its hardware and software may, for instance, let it serve as a stopwatch or an alarm clock. They may let you check the time or date, do arithmetic, or make notes about things you don't want to forget. Many phones have games and let you take pictures and make videos. Some can tell you the meanings of foreign words.

Powerful phones like this one are especially good for playing games.

Beyond the Phone

For many applications, you need services outside the phone. This might be the telephone network, the Internet, or something else. To make a phone call or send a text message, for example, you have to use the telephone network or the Internet. Outside services also make it possible to do many other things. If your phone has the right hardware and software, you may be able to do your e-mail, receive news updates, and surf the Web. You might also be able to watch television, play games with others, or get and send music, pictures, and videos.

A boy takes aim in a 2008 U.S. cell phone-throwing competition.

DID YOU KNOW ?

Long Distance

One application doesn't need any software or outside source. The sport of cell phone throwing uses only the hardware. There are two types of throw: traditional (over the shoulder) and freestyle. World championships take place each summer in northern Europe. At the 2008 event, held in the country of Estonia, the best throw in the traditional style went 280 feet (85 meters).

Cell Safety

Carelessness with cell phones can lead to problems. For instance, some parts of a phone, such as the battery, contain poisonous materials. They can be a danger if the phone gets thrown away. They may leak out when the trash is burned or buried in a landfill. For this reason, it is a good idea to recycle unwanted phones or find new owners for them. Some phone companies accept used phones. Don't forget to remove your personal information, such as names and phone numbers, from the phone before you recycle it.

Recycling old phones lets the materials in them be reused and also helps the environment.

Using a phone while doing something else can sometimes be risky. You may not be able to give that other task the attention it deserves. Someone texting while crossing the street can't watch out for traffic. Someone talking on the phone while driving a car may not be able to pay enough attention to what's happening on the road. In some areas it is even against the law to use a cell phone while driving.

Cell Phone Viruses

Viruses that harm cell phone software may become a problem. The first known cell phone virus, called Cabir, showed up in 2004. So far, though, these viruses are not common.

Radio waves from a cell phone are another concern. They might interfere with some equipment or wireless networks. So cell phones may need to be turned off in certain hospital areas. On airplanes in the United States and some other countries, cell phones must be off when the plane is in flight.

DID YOU KNOW ?

Phones and Health

Cell phones give off radio waves. Some people worry that this radiation could cause health problems. Scientists have been studying the issue. At this point, there is no cause for alarm.

Doing More and More

New ways to use cell phones keep popping up. In some countries you can buy drinks or snacks from vending machines using your cell phone. (The cost is added to your phone bill or charged to a credit card.) In 2007 a college in Japan started teaching a course over cell phones. Around the same time, some airlines began to let people use their cell phone to get on planes. Passengers no longer had to use a paper boarding pass. Instead, they showed a special code on their phone's screen. Today, some people use their cell phones to call home to turn on the oven, or switch on the lights, or turn on the air conditioning so that the house will be cool when they arrive home.

In some places you can buy things from a vending machine with your cell phone.

New Features All the Time

Meanwhile, phone makers keep adding new features to their phones. The first handset, in 1973, was big and couldn't do much. Just a little over 30 years later, phones began to come out that had an FM **transmitter**. This let you send music stored on your phone to a nearby radio.

In 2007 a company in Japan came up with a cell phone that helps keep track of the user's health. It can tell whether you are walking, running, or resting and count how many calories you are burning. In addition, it uses infrared to measure your pulse rate. A gas sensor in the phone even lets you know if you have bad breath.

Some airlines let you use a smart phone instead of a paper boarding pass.

What Is NFC?

NFC is one way cell phones may become more useful. The name stands for "Near Field Communications." NFC uses radio waves to link up with other devices in order to exchange information. It works at very short distances. A cell phone with NFC could be used like a credit card or might serve as an identity card, like a passport. It might also be used to lock and unlock doors. If you happen to see a poster advertising something you find interesting, the poster might be able to send details to your NFC cell phone.

Glossary

analog—A name for one type of electric signal that carries information. Analog signals are similar in pattern (analogous) to their source.

base station—The site that cell phones link up with to make telephone calls. It has an antenna. There is one base station in each **cell** area.

cell—A small area in which all cell phones connect with a single site called a **base station**.

chip—A little piece of material that contains tiny devices such as transistors for processing electric signals.

digital—A name for one type of electric signal that carries information. With digital signals, the original information is chopped up into tiny bits.

electromagnetic radiation—A way that energy moves through space as waves. Radio waves are one type. Light is another. **Infrared** is still another.

frequency—The number of ups and downs a wave makes each second. It is measured in cycles per second, or **hertz**.

handset—The part of a telephone that you hold in your hand. With traditional telephones, the handset is connected to another part of the phone. With cell phones, the handset contains the entire phone.

hertz—A way of describing the frequency of waves. One hertz is one full cycle—one up and down beat—of a wave each second. Two hertz is two cycles each second. Large numbers of hertz have special names. For instance, 1,000 hertz is 1 kilohertz, 1 million hertz is 1 megahertz, and 1 billion hertz is 1 gigahertz.

infrared—A type of **electromagnetic radiation**. It is like light but cannot be seen.

landline phone—A phone that uses a wire to link to the phone **network**.

network—A group of devices that are linked together, such as telephones.

receiver—A device that receives signals, such as radio waves.

smart phone—A cell phone that not only makes calls but has some features like a computer.

transistor—A tiny device that can change electric signals in useful ways.

transmitter—A device that sends radio waves.

walkie-talkie—A combination radio **receiver** and **transmitter** that you can hold in your hand. Unlike a telephone, a walkie-talkie lets you do only one thing at a time. You either talk or listen.

To Learn More

Read these books:

Cunningham, Kevin. *Cell Phones*. Ann Arbor, Mich.: Cherry Lake, 2008.

Kelby, Scott, and Terry White. *The iPhone Book*. Berkeley, Calif.: Peachpit, 2007.

Stefoff, Rebecca. *The Telephone*. New York: Benchmark, 2005.

Woodford, Chris. *Cool Stuff Exploded*. New York: Dorling Kindersley, 2008.

Look up these Web sites:

CBC (Canadian Broadcasting Corporation)
http://www.cbc.ca/doczone/cellphones

Environmental Protection Agency, The Life Cycle of a Cell Phone
http://www.epa.gov/epawaste/index.htm

Federal Communications Commission, Kids Zone
http://www.fcc.gov/cgb/kidszone/faqs_cellphones.html

How Stuff Works
http://electronics.howstuffworks.com/cell-phone.htm

Mobile Phone Throwing World Championships
http://www.savonlinnafestivals.com/en_index.htm

Key Internet search terms:

cell phone, mobile phone, radio waves, telephone

Index

About the Author

Richard Hantula has written, edited, and translated books and articles on science and technology for more than three decades. He was the senior U.S. editor for the *Macmillan Encyclopedia of Science*.